Journaling Through Creation with God

ISBN: 979-8-9910491-0-8

Scripture quotations are taken from

THE HOLY BIBLE, NEW INTERNATIONAL VERSION®, NIV© Copyright © 1973, 1978, 1984, 2011 by Biblica, Inc.® Used by permission. All rights reserved worldwide.

Cover design and layout formatting by Nelly Murariu at PixBeeDesign.com.

Graphics from Canva

Journaling Through Creation with God

A Spiritual Journey of Creativity

Robin Simpson

Dedication

To Malachi Charis, my little Messenger of Grace. God surely gave us you as a reminder of what is ultimately important - spending eternity with our heavenly Father.

CONTENTS

Introduction

Welcome to *Journaling Through Creation with God*! I am so glad you chose to begin this 30-day transformative journey. This reflective, interactive journal invites you to develop a renewed awareness of God's miraculous creativity. Each day's activity will guide you through reading, scripture writing, specific attributes of God, praise, prayer and nature discoveries. Your spirit will be refreshed daily as you intentionally encounter God in creation.

The Bible study method is developed from Deuteronomy 17:18-19. This advice was given to the incoming king: "When he takes the throne of his kingdom, he is to write for himself on a scroll a copy of this law, taken from that of the Levitical priests. It is to be with him, and he is to read it all the days of his life so that he may learn to revere the Lord his God and follow carefully all the words of this law and these decrees." If it was so important for a king to read the Scriptures, write them out for himself, learn to revere God, and follow the Scriptures carefully, surely it carries significance for us too.

How to Use This Journal

This journal can be used as a creative scrapbooking or journaling opportunity or simply as a Bible study where you fill in the blanks with your descriptive words.

Each day contains these features:

 READ: Begin by reading today's passage in Scripture.

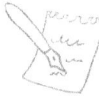 **WRITE:** Write out the selected verses from today's reading. If you feel you don't have sufficient space, you have the opportunity to be creative and write or print them out on a separate paper and glue them in your journal. The purpose is to thoughtfully interact with the text of God's word in whichever way you choose.

 **LEARN:** What do you learn simply and specifically about God just from these verses? For example, if the passage is Genesis 1:1-8, here are some ideas of what you might learn from these verses:

† God was there in the beginning

† God is the creator

† In the beginning God created both the heavens and the earth

† When God spoke and said, "Let there be light" there was light

† God saw that the light was good

† God separated the light from the darkness

† God named the day and the night

† God created the first evening and morning

† When God spoke and said, "Let there be a vault between the waters to separate water from water," it was so

† God named the sky.

 REVERE: In this section, you will fill in the blanks using a synonym of the word "revere" (admire, adore, appreciate, cherish, exalt, honor, respect, praise, worship) and complete the following sentences explaining how you praise or revere God from what you learned today.

For example:

1. God, I *worship* you because *you created the heavens and the earth.*

2. God, I *exalt* you because *you alone are God.*

3. God, I *admire* you because *when I go out at night and look up at the sky, I see the beauty of the work of your hands in the stars above.*

 **FOLLOW:** Every day gives you the opportunity to follow God more closely and deepen your relationship with him by actively and intentionally experiencing his creation. In this section, you can choose to write down and describe in detail (or draw, color, or scrapbook) one or more of the following: something you can see, something you can hear, something you can touch, something you can smell, or something you can taste that you are thankful to God for creating.

Note: There are some "Be Creative" blank pages at the end of the journal if you would like to test out your colored pencils, pens, markers, or other supplies before you begin.

 PRAYER: Here you will continue your own conversation with God with a prayer that has been started for you.

 **NATURE DISCOVERY:** This section invites you to add something to your nature pocket and log it so you can remember what you chose and why.

Today I added .... to my nature pocket to remind me of God. I chose it because ....

....

....

How to create a nature pocket for your discoveries:

A nature pocket is a place where you can collect and keep your small discoveries (such as pressed leaves, flowers, stones, seeds, shells, feathers, etc.) that remind you of your wonderful Creator. A nature pocket can be created from any kind of container. You could use a small box, a sealable plastic bag, a mailing envelope, a jar, etc. If something is too large to add, you might consider creating a texture rubbing of it. To create a texture rubbing, lay a piece of paper over the object, hold the paper firmly in place, and use the side of a crayon to rub over the top of the paper and object until you see the texture lines come through; this way you still have a reminder of your discovery for the day!

Alternative digital nature pocket: Take a picture of what you find, write a caption on it, and save it to a nature pocket photo album you create on your phone or computer.

It's my prayer that over the next 30 days, *Journaling Through Creation with God* will uplift your spirit and guide you into a deeper relationship with your heavenly Father as you intentionally encounter him every day.

To download your free nature pocket cover sheet and access other ideas and tips for using this journal as a creation scrapbook, visit www.calledtobehis.com or click on the code below.

WEEK ONE

In the Beginning God Created the Heavens and the Earth

"By the word of the Lord the heavens were made, their starry host by the breath of his mouth. He gathers the waters of the sea into jars; he puts the deep into storehouses. Let all the earth fear the Lord; let all the people of the world revere him. For he spoke, and it came to be; he commanded, and it stood firm."

Psalm 33:6-9

"By faith we understand that the universe was formed at God's command, so that what is seen was not made out of what was visible."

Hebrews 11:3

Day One

 READ: Begin today by reading Genesis 1:1-8 in your Bible.

WRITE: Write Genesis 1:1-8 here:

....

....

....

....

....

....

....

....

....

....

....

....

....

....

LEARN: What do you learn simply and specifically about God just from these verses? Write your observations here:

....

....

....

....

....

....

REVERE: Fill in the blanks using a synonym of the word "revere" (admire, adore, appreciate, cherish, exalt, honor, respect, praise, worship) and complete the following sentences explaining how you praise or revere God from what you learned today.

1. God, I .... you because ....

....

2. God, I .... you because ....

....

3. God, I .... you because ....

....

FOLLOW: Every day gives you the opportunity to follow God more closely and deepen your relationship with him by actively and intentionally experiencing his creation.

In the space below, write down and describe in detail (or draw, color, or scrapbook) one or more of the following: something you can see, something you can hear, something you can touch, something you can smell, or something you can taste that you are thankful to God for creating.

CONTINUE THIS PRAYER WITH YOUR OWN CONVERSATION WITH GOD:

Dear God, thank you for creating the heavens and the earth. Thank you for creating that first day, that first evening and morning, and thank you for letting your creation renew itself everyday by displaying your majesty in the skies.

....

....

....

....

....

....

....

.... *Amen.*

NATURE DISCOVERY: Today I added .... to my nature pocket to remind me of God. I chose it because

....

....

....

....

....

....

Day Two

 READ: Begin today by reading Genesis 1:9-19 in your Bible.

WRITE: Write Genesis 1:9-19 here:

....

....

....

....

....

....

....

....

....

....

....

....

....

....

LEARN: What do you learn simply and specifically about God just from these verses? Write your observations here:

....

....

....

....

....

....

REVERE: Fill in the blanks using a synonym of the word "revere" (admire, adore, appreciate, cherish, exalt, honor, respect, praise, worship) and complete the following sentences explaining how you praise or revere God from what you learned today.

1. God, I .... you because ....

....

2. God, I .... you because ....

....

3. God, I .... you because ....

....

FOLLOW: Every day gives you the opportunity to follow God more closely and deepen your relationship with him by actively and intentionally experiencing his creation.

In the space below, write down and describe in detail (or draw, color, or scrapbook) one or more of the following: something you can see, something you can hear, something you can touch, something you can smell, or something you can taste that you are thankful to God for creating.

CONTINUE THIS PRAYER WITH YOUR OWN CONVERSATION WITH GOD:

Dear God, thank you for making our world such a beautiful place to live! Thank you for the variety of the landscapes with mountains, plains, and beaches, for the lakes and rivers and seas. Thank you for the tall trees, the rainbow colors of the flowers, and the powerful rhythmic sounds of crashing waves. What an awesome creative God you are. ....

....

....

....

....

....

....

.... *Amen.*

NATURE DISCOVERY: Today I added ....
to my nature pocket to remind me of God. I chose it because

....

....

....

....

....

Day Three

 READ: Begin today by reading Genesis 1:20-25 in your Bible.

WRITE: Write Genesis 1:20-25 here:

....

....

....

....

....

....

....

....

....

....

....

....

....

....

LEARN: What do you learn simply and specifically about God just from these verses? Write your observations here:

....

....

....

....

....

....

REVERE: Fill in the blanks using a synonym of the word "revere" (admire, adore, appreciate, cherish, exalt, honor, respect, praise, worship) and complete the following sentences explaining how you praise or revere God from what you learned today.

1. God, I .... you because ....

....

2. God, I .... you because ....

....

3. God, I .... you because ....

....

FOLLOW: Every day gives you the opportunity to follow God more closely and deepen your relationship with him by actively and intentionally experiencing his creation.

In the space below, write down and describe in detail (or draw, color, or scrapbook) one or more of the following: something you can see, something you can hear, something you can touch, something you can smell, or something you can taste that you are thankful to God for creating.

CONTINUE THIS PRAYER WITH YOUR OWN CONVERSATION WITH GOD:

Dear God, what a breathtaking God you are! From the majestic eagle in the sky, to the speeding cheetah on the savannah, to the playful dolphins in the sea, I am thrilled with every beautiful, complex design of your remarkable animals. Lord, I praise you for the creative and imaginative God that you are, for ....

....

....

....

....

....

.... *Amen.*

NATURE DISCOVERY: Today I added .... to my nature pocket to remind me of God. I chose it because

....

....

....

....

....

....

Day Four

 READ: Begin today by reading Isaiah 45 in your Bible.

WRITE: Write Isaiah 45:7-8, 12, 18 here:

....

....

....

....

....

....

....

....

....

....

....

....

....

....

LEARN: What do you learn simply and specifically about God just from these verses? Write your observations here:

....

....

....

....

....

....

REVERE: Fill in the blanks using a synonym of the word "revere" (admire, adore, appreciate, cherish, exalt, honor, respect, praise, worship) and complete the following sentences explaining how you praise or revere God from what you learned today.

1. God, I .... you because ....

....

2. God, I .... you because ....

....

3. God, I .... you because ....

....

FOLLOW: Every day gives you the opportunity to follow God more closely and deepen your relationship with him by actively and intentionally experiencing his creation.

In the space below, write down and describe in detail (or draw, color, or scrapbook) one or more of the following: something you can see, something you can hear, something you can touch, something you can smell, or something you can taste that you are thankful to God for creating.

CONTINUE THIS PRAYER WITH YOUR OWN CONVERSATION WITH GOD:

Dear God, I stand amazed at the power of your hands that can stretch out the heavens and their starry hosts! I praise you for your plan of creation, that you planned for the world not to be empty, but to be inhabited. Thank you for letting us enjoy the world that you have created. ....

....

....

....

....

....

.... *Amen.*

NATURE DISCOVERY: Today I added ....
to my nature pocket to remind me of God. I chose it because

....

....

....

....

....

....

Day Five

 READ: Begin today by reading Colossians 1:1-23 in your Bible.

WRITE: Write Colossians 1:15-17 here:

....

....

....

....

....

....

....

....

....

....

....

....

....

....

LEARN: What do you learn simply and specifically about God just from these verses? Write your observations here:

....

....

....

....

....

....

REVERE: Fill in the blanks using a synonym of the word "revere" (admire, adore, appreciate, cherish, exalt, honor, respect, praise, worship) and complete the following sentences explaining how you praise or revere God from what you learned today.

1. God, I .... you because ....

....

2. God, I .... you because ....

....

3. God, I .... you because ....

....

FOLLOW: Every day gives you the opportunity to follow God more closely and deepen your relationship with him by actively and intentionally experiencing his creation.

In the space below, write down and describe in detail (or draw, color, or scrapbook) one or more of the following: something you can see, something you can hear, something you can touch, something you can smell, or something you can taste that you are thankful to God for creating.

CONTINUE THIS PRAYER WITH YOUR OWN CONVERSATION WITH GOD:

Dear God, thank you for your Son! Thank you for holding all things, including me, together! Thank you for letting him make peace for me through his blood that was shed on the cross. ....

....

....

....

....

....

....

.... *Amen.*

NATURE DISCOVERY: Today I added ....
to my nature pocket to remind me of God. I chose it because

....

....

....

....

....

....

....

The earth is the Lord's, and everything in it, the world, and all who live in it; for he founded it on the seas and established it on the waters.

Psalm 24:1-2

WEEK TWO

Creation's Response: All Creation Sings Praises to God

"Praise the Lord. Praise the Lord from the heavens; praise him in the heights above. Praise him, all his angels; praise him, all his heavenly hosts. Praise him, sun and moon; praise him, all you shining stars. Praise him, you highest heavens and you waters above the skies. Let them praise the name of the Lord, for at his command they were created, and he established them for ever and ever – he issued a decree that will never pass away."

Psalm 148:1-6

Day One

 READ: Begin today by reading Psalm 19 in your Bible.

WRITE: Write Psalm 19:1-4 here:

....

....

....

....

....

....

....

....

....

....

....

....

....

....

LEARN: What do you learn simply and specifically about God and creation's praise of him just from these verses? Write your observations here:

....

....

....

....

....

....

REVERE: Fill in the blanks using a synonym of the word "revere" (admire, adore, appreciate, cherish, exalt, honor, respect, praise, worship) and complete the following sentences explaining how you praise or revere God from what you learned today.

1. God, I .... you because ....

....

2. God, I .... you because ....

....

3. God, I .... you because ....

....

FOLLOW: Every day gives you the opportunity to follow God more closely and deepen your relationship with him by actively and intentionally experiencing his creation.

In the space below, write down and describe in detail (or draw, color, paint or scrapbook) one or more of the following: something you can see, something you can hear, something you can touch, something you can smell, or something you can taste that you are thankful to God for creating.

CONTINUE THIS PRAYER WITH YOUR OWN CONVERSATION WITH GOD:

Dear God, I look outside today and see how the heavens are declaring your glory this morning through the rays of sunlight appearing over the horizon! I am so thankful that you thought to include beauty in the skies as dusk turns into dawn

....

....

....

....

....

....

....

.... *Amen.*

NATURE DISCOVERY: Today I added ....
to my nature pocket to remind me of God. I chose it because

....

....

....

....

....

....

....

Day Two

 **READ:** Begin today by reading Psalm 65 in your Bible.

WRITE: Write Psalm 65:8, 12, 13 here:

....

....

....

....

....

....

....

....

....

....

....

....

....

....

LEARN: What do you learn simply and specifically about God and creation's praise of him just from these verses? Write your observations here:

....

....

....

....

....

....

REVERE: Fill in the blanks using a synonym of the word "revere" (admire, adore, appreciate, cherish, exalt, honor, respect, praise, worship) and complete the following sentences explaining how you praise or revere God from what you learned today.

1. God, I .... you because ....

....

2. God, I .... you because ....

....

3. God, I .... you because ....

....

FOLLOW: Every day gives you the opportunity to follow God more closely and deepen your relationship with him by actively and intentionally experiencing his creation.

In the space below, write down and describe in detail (or draw, color, paint or scrapbook) one or more of the following: something you can see, something you can hear, something you can touch, something you can smell, or something you can taste that you are thankful to God for creating.

CONTINUE THIS PRAYER WITH YOUR OWN CONVERSATION WITH GOD:

Dear God, the whole earth is filled with admiration at your wonders and I praise you! I praise you for creation's joyful songs that I hear when I simply stop and look and listen. From the grasslands to the hills, from the meadows to the valleys they all shout for joy and sing of your majesty ....

....

....

....

....

....

....*Amen.*

NATURE DISCOVERY: Today I added ....
to my nature pocket to remind me of God. I chose it because

....

....

....

....

....

....

....

Day Three

READ: Begin today by reading Psalm 96 in your Bible.

WRITE: Write Psalm 96:1-4, 11-14 here:

....

....

....

....

....

....

....

....

....

....

....

....

....

....

LEARN: What do you learn simply and specifically about God and creation's praise of him just from these verses? Write your observations here:

....

....

....

....

....

....

REVERE: Fill in the blanks using a synonym of the word "revere" (admire, adore, appreciate, cherish, exalt, honor, respect, praise, worship) and complete the following sentences explaining how you praise or revere God from what you learned today.

1. God, I .... you because ....

....

2. God, I .... you because ....

....

3. God, I .... you because ....

....

FOLLOW: Every day gives you the opportunity to follow God more closely and deepen your relationship with him by actively and intentionally experiencing his creation.

In the space below, write down and describe in detail (or draw, color, paint or scrapbook) one or more of the following: something you can see, something you can hear, something you can touch, something you can smell, or something you can taste that you are thankful to God for creating.

CONTINUE THIS PRAYER WITH YOUR OWN CONVERSATION WITH GOD:

Dear God, how marvelous it is that your creation expresses emotion! The heavens rejoice, the earth is glad, the sea resounds, the fields are jubilant, and the trees of the forest all sing for joy to you our Lord and God! I also praise you and sing to you with my heart and my voice as I consider the work of your hands

....

....

....

....

....

....

.... *Amen.*

NATURE DISCOVERY: Today I added ....
to my nature pocket to remind me of God. I chose it because

....

....

....

....

....

Day Four

 READ: Begin today by reading Psalm 98 in your Bible.

WRITE: Write Psalm 98:4-9 here:

....

....

....

....

....

....

....

....

....

....

....

....

....

....

LEARN: What do you learn simply and specifically about God and creation's praise of him just from these verses? Write your observations here:

....

....

....

....

....

....

REVERE: Fill in the blanks using a synonym of the word "revere" (admire, adore, appreciate, cherish, exalt, honor, respect, praise, worship) and complete the following sentences explaining how you praise or revere God from what you learned today.

1. God, I .... you because ....

....

2. God, I .... you because ....

....

3. God, I .... you because ....

....

FOLLOW: Every day gives you the opportunity to follow God more closely and deepen your relationship with him by actively and intentionally experiencing his creation.

In the space below, write down and describe in detail (or draw, color, paint or scrapbook) one or more of the following: something you can see, something you can hear, something you can touch, something you can smell, or something you can taste that you are thankful to God for creating.

CONTINUE THIS PRAYER WITH YOUR OWN CONVERSATION WITH GOD:

Dear God, I love how the psalmist begins Psalm 98, "Sing to the Lord a new song, for he has done marvelous things; …" and indeed you have! Your deeds are so marvelous that your creation praises you: the sea, the world, those in the world, the rivers, and the mountains. God, please forgive me when I take your creation for granted and help me to open my eyes to see and hear all the marvelous things that you have done ....

....

....

....

....

....

.... *Amen.*

NATURE DISCOVERY: Today I added .... to my nature pocket to remind me of God. I chose it because

....

....

....

....

....

....

Day Five

 READ: Begin today by reading Psalm 148 in your Bible.

WRITE: Write Psalm 148:7-14 here:

....

....

....

....

....

....

....

....

....

....

....

....

....

....

LEARN: What do you learn simply and specifically about God and creation's praise of him just from these verses? Write your observations here:

....

....

....

....

....

....

REVERE: Fill in the blanks using a synonym of the word "revere" (admire, adore, appreciate, cherish, exalt, honor, respect, praise, worship) and complete the following sentences explaining how you praise or revere God from what you learned today.

1. God, I .... you because ....

....

2. God, I .... you because ....

....

3. God, I .... you because ....

....

FOLLOW: Every day gives you the opportunity to follow God more closely and deepen your relationship with him by actively and intentionally experiencing his creation.

In the space below, write down and describe in detail (or draw, color, paint or scrapbook) one or more of the following: something you can see, something you can hear, something you can touch, something you can smell, or something you can taste that you are thankful to God for creating.

CONTINUE THIS PRAYER WITH YOUR OWN CONVERSATION WITH GOD:

Dear God, when I go outside and just listen, I hear your creation praising you and bringing glory to your name. I hear the gentle wind rustling the leaves on the trees, I hear birds singing their melodious songs, I hear the river gurgling over the rocks and waterfalls, I hear and I praise your name too. ....

....

....

....

....

....

.... *Amen.*

NATURE DISCOVERY: Today I added .... to my nature pocket to remind me of God. I chose it because

....

....

....

....

....

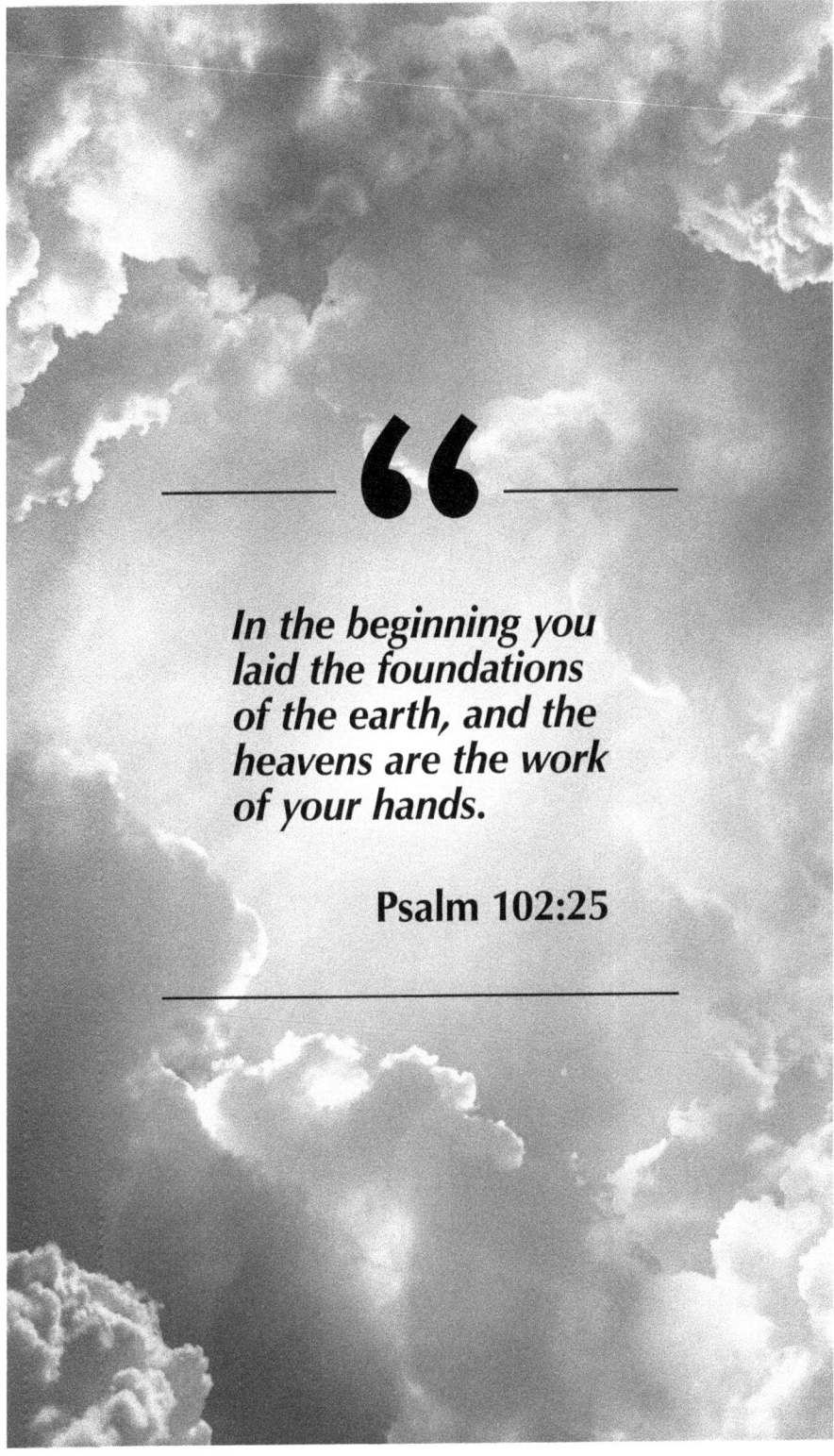

In the beginning you laid the foundations of the earth, and the heavens are the work of your hands.

Psalm 102:25

WEEK THREE

God Created Us

"When God created mankind, he made them in the likeness of God. He created them male and female and blessed them. And he named them "Mankind" when they were created."

Genesis 5:1-2

Day One

 **READ:** Begin today by reading Genesis 1:26-31 in your Bible.

WRITE: Write Genesis 1:26-31 here:

....

....

....

....

....

....

....

....

....

....

....

....

....

....

LEARN: What do you learn simply and specifically about God and creation's praise of him just from these verses? Write your observations here:

....

....

....

....

....

....

REVERE: Fill in the blanks using a synonym of the word "revere" (admire, adore, appreciate, cherish, exalt, honor, respect, praise, worship) and complete the following sentences explaining how you praise or revere God from what you learned today.

1. God, I .... you because ....

....

2. God, I .... you because ....

....

3. God, I .... you because ....

....

FOLLOW: Every day gives you the opportunity to follow God more closely and deepen your relationship with him by actively and intentionally experiencing his creation.

In the space below, write down and describe in detail (or draw, color, paint or scrapbook) one or more of the following: something you can see, something you can hear, something you can touch, something you can smell, or something you can taste that you are thankful to God for creating.

CONTINUE THIS PRAYER WITH YOUR OWN CONVERSATION WITH GOD:

Dear God, you are my heavenly Father. How humbled and blessed I am to be made in your image! Your remarkable creativity never ceases to amaze me. When I consider the variety of plants, some to eat and satisfy our hunger, others to heal our bodies, and some simply for our visual enjoyment, I am amazed at how thoughtful and intentional you are in your creation. I often take these for granted, and I want to thank you for creating them all with a purpose! .... is one of my favorite vegetables and .... is one of my favorite fruits! I also enjoy having .... from your creation because

....

....

....

....

....

.... *Amen.*

NATURE DISCOVERY: Today I added ....
to my nature pocket to remind me of God. I chose it because

....

....

....

....

....

Day Two

 READ: Begin today by reading Psalm 139 in your Bible.

WRITE: Write Psalm 139:13-18 here:

....

....

....

....

....

....

....

....

....

....

....

....

....

....

LEARN: What do you learn simply and specifically about God and creation's praise of him just from these verses? Write your observations here:

....

....

....

....

....

....

REVERE: Fill in the blanks using a synonym of the word "revere" (admire, adore, appreciate, cherish, exalt, honor, respect, praise, worship) and complete the following sentences explaining how you praise or revere God from what you learned today.

1. God, I .... you because ....

....

2. God, I .... you because ....

....

3. God, I .... you because ....

....

FOLLOW: Every day gives you the opportunity to follow God more closely and deepen your relationship with him by actively and intentionally experiencing his creation.

In the space below, write down and describe in detail (or draw, color, paint or scrapbook) one or more of the following: something you can see, something you can hear, something you can touch, something you can smell, or something you can taste that you are thankful to God for creating.

CONTINUE THIS PRAYER WITH YOUR OWN CONVERSATION WITH GOD:

Dear God, you are my heavenly Father and you know me better than anyone, better than I even know myself! Anywhere I go you are already there and for that I am so thankful! You know my thoughts, my anxieties, my successes, my failures, and yet you still love me. Please use your wisdom about me and guide me

....

....

....

....

....

....

.... *Amen.*

NATURE DISCOVERY: Today I added ....
to my nature pocket to remind me of God. I chose it because

....

....

....

....

....

....

....

Day Three

 READ: Begin today by reading Isaiah 42 in your Bible.

Write: Write Isaiah 42:5-7 here:

....

....

....

....

....

....

....

....

....

....

....

....

....

....

LEARN: What do you learn simply and specifically about God and creation's praise of him just from these verses? Write your observations here:

....

....

....

....

....

....

REVERE: Fill in the blanks using a synonym of the word "revere" (admire, adore, appreciate, cherish, exalt, honor, respect, praise, worship) and complete the following sentences explaining how you praise or revere God from what you learned today.

1. God, I .... you because ....

....

2. God, I .... you because ....

....

3. God, I .... you because ....

....

FOLLOW: Every day gives you the opportunity to follow God more closely and deepen your relationship with him by actively and intentionally experiencing his creation.

In the space below, write down and describe in detail (or draw, color, paint or scrapbook) one or more of the following: something you can see, something you can hear, something you can touch, something you can smell, or something you can taste that you are thankful to God for creating.

CONTINUE THIS PRAYER WITH YOUR OWN CONVERSATION WITH GOD:

Dear God, you are my heavenly Father. I am so thankful for the breath of life that you gave me! I am so amazed to have been created in your image. Lord, you have called me in righteousness; help me to hold on to your hand and be a shining light to other people so that they too can come to know you ....

....

....

....

....

....

.... *Amen.*

NATURE DISCOVERY: Today I added .... to my nature pocket to remind me of God. I chose it because

....

....

....

....

....

....

....

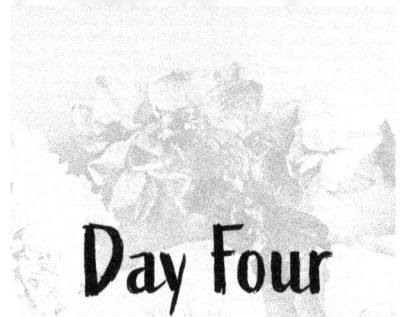

Day Four

 READ: Begin today by reading Isaiah 44 in your Bible.

WRITE: Write Isaiah 44:2, 24 here:

....

....

....

....

....

....

....

....

....

....

....

....

....

....

LEARN: What do you learn simply and specifically about God and creation's praise of him just from these verses? Write your observations here:

....

....

....

....

....

....

REVERE: Fill in the blanks using a synonym of the word "revere" (admire, adore, appreciate, cherish, exalt, honor, respect, praise, worship) and complete the following sentences explaining how you praise or revere God from what you learned today.

1. God, I .... you because ....

....

2. God, I .... you because ....

....

3. God, I .... you because ....

....

FOLLOW: Every day gives you the opportunity to follow God more closely and deepen your relationship with him by actively and intentionally experiencing his creation.

In the space below, write down and describe in detail (or draw, color, paint or scrapbook) one or more of the following: something you can see, something you can hear, something you can touch, something you can smell, or something you can taste that you are thankful to God for creating.

CONTINUE THIS PRAYER WITH YOUR OWN CONVERSATION WITH GOD:

Dear God, you are my heavenly Father. Thank you for being my Creator and my Redeemer! Thank you ....

....

....

....

....

....

.... *Amen.*

NATURE DISCOVERY: Today I added ....
to my nature pocket to remind me of God. I chose it because

....

....

....

....

....

....

....

Day Five

 READ: Begin today by reading Ephesians 2:10 and Ephesians 4:17-32 in your Bible.

WRITE: Write Ephesians 2:10 and 4:22-24 here:

....

....

....

....

....

....

....

....

....

....

....

....

....

....

LEARN: What do you learn simply and specifically about God and creation's praise of him just from these verses? Write your observations here:

....

....

....

....

....

....

REVERE: Fill in the blanks using a synonym of the word "revere" (admire, adore, appreciate, cherish, exalt, honor, respect, praise, worship) and complete the following sentences explaining how you praise or revere God from what you learned today.

1. God, I .... you because ....

....

2. God, I .... you because ....

....

3. God, I .... you because ....

....

FOLLOW: Every day gives you the opportunity to follow God more closely and deepen your relationship with him by actively and intentionally experiencing his creation.

In the space below, write down and describe in detail (or draw, color, paint or scrapbook) one or more of the following: something you can see, something you can hear, something you can touch, something you can smell, or something you can taste that you are thankful to God for creating.

CONTINUE THIS PRAYER WITH YOUR OWN CONVERSATION WITH GOD:

Dear God, you are my heavenly Father. Although I am made in your image, I am still human and I make mistakes and I sin. Thank you for sending your Son to make me alive again through your grace! I am your workmanship; I am created in Christ Jesus to do good works. Please open my eyes to see the good things you have planned for me to do, open my ears to hear your words, open my heart to respond when you call me and open my hands and feet to go and to respond. Help me to put on my new self every day and remember ....

....

....

....

....

....

.... *Amen.*

NATURE DISCOVERY: Today I added .... to my nature pocket to remind me of God. I chose it because

....

....

....

....

....

....

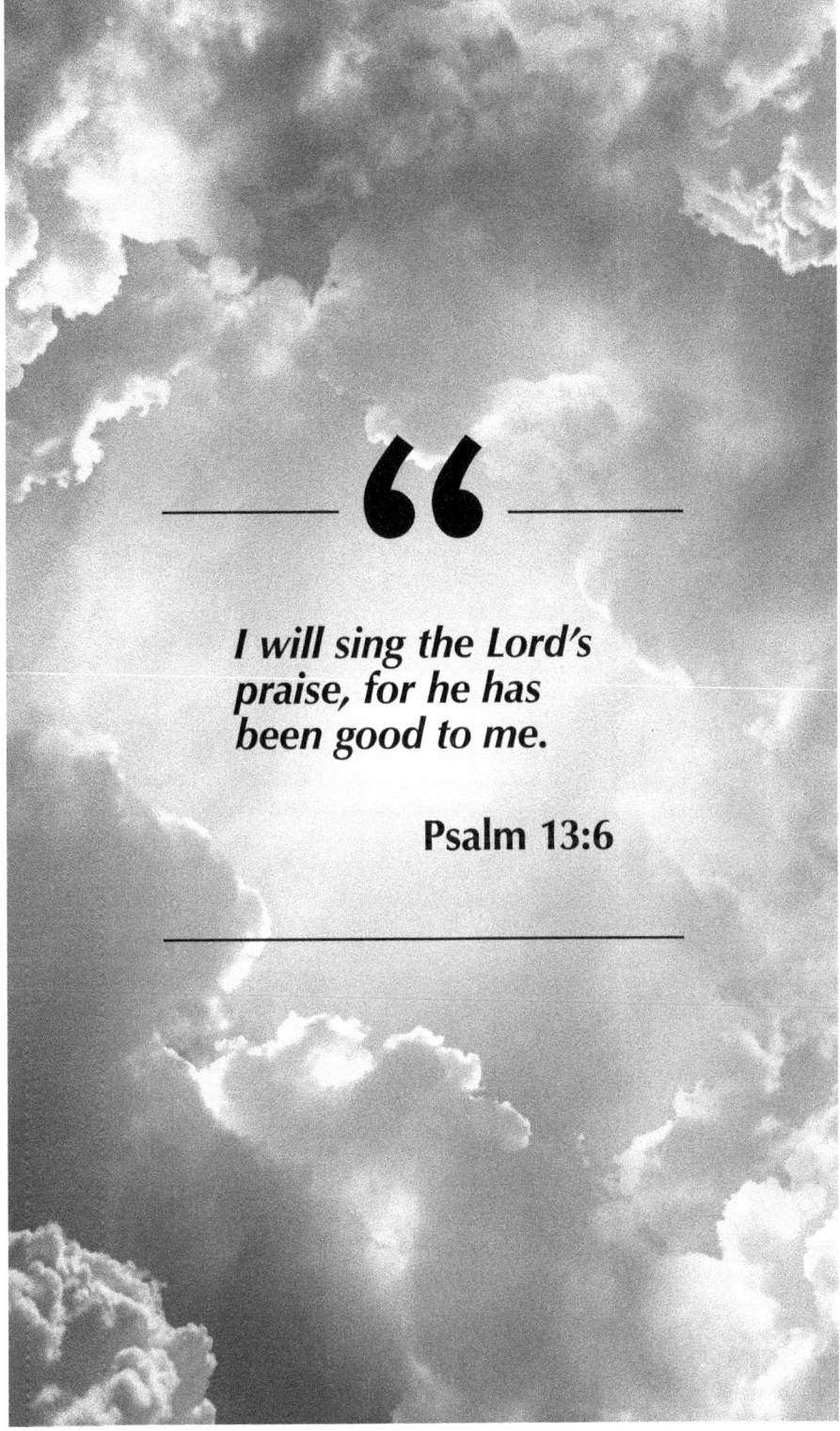

I will sing the Lord's praise, for he has been good to me.

Psalm 13:6

WEEK FOUR

Our Response: We Sing Praises to God

"Sing praises to God, sing praises;
sing praises to our King, sing praises.
For God is the King of all the earth;
sing to him a psalm of praise."

Psalm 47:6

"I will praise you, Lord, among the
nations; I will sing of you among
the peoples. For great is your
love, reaching to the heavens; your
faithfulness reaches to the skies. Be
exalted, O God, above the heavens;
let your glory be over all the earth."

Psalm 57:9-11

"But I will sing of your strength, in
the morning I will sing of your love;
for you are my fortress, my refuge in
times of trouble. You are my strength,
I sing praise to you; you, God, are my
fortress, my God on whom I can rely."

Psalm 59:16-17

Day One

 **READ:** Begin today by reading Psalm 9 in your Bible.

WRITE: Write Psalm 9:1-2, 11 here:

....

....

....

....

....

....

....

....

....

....

....

....

....

LEARN: What do you learn simply and specifically about God and creation's praise of him just from these verses? Write your observations here:

....

....

....

....

....

....

REVERE: Fill in the blanks using a synonym of the word "revere" (admire, adore, appreciate, cherish, exalt, honor, respect, praise, worship) and complete the following sentences explaining how you praise or revere God from what you learned today.

1. God, I .... you because ....

....

2. God, I .... you because ....

....

3. God, I .... you because ....

....

FOLLOW: Every day gives you the opportunity to follow God more closely and deepen your relationship with him by actively and intentionally experiencing his creation.

In the space below, write down and describe in detail (or draw, color, paint or scrapbook) one or more of the following: something you can see, something you can hear, something you can touch, something you can smell, or something you can taste that you are thankful to God for creating.

CONTINUE THIS PRAYER WITH YOUR OWN CONVERSATION WITH GOD:

Dear God, you are my heavenly Father. I want to praise you with all my heart and sing praises to your name, O Most High! Lord, I rejoice in you and my heart is happy when I can share you with others. Please give me courage to ....

....

....

....

....

....

....

.... *Amen.*

NATURE DISCOVERY: Today I added ....
to my nature pocket to remind me of God. I chose it because

....

....

....

....

....

....

....

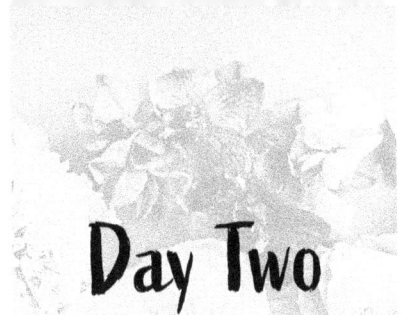

Day Two

 READ: Begin today by reading Psalm 95 in your Bible.

WRITE: Write Psalm 95:1-7 here:

....

....

....

....

....

....

....

....

....

....

....

....

....

....

LEARN: What do you learn simply and specifically about God and creation's praise of him just from these verses? Write your observations here:

....

....

....

....

....

....

REVERE: Fill in the blanks using a synonym of the word "revere" (admire, adore, appreciate, cherish, exalt, honor, respect, praise, worship) and complete the following sentences explaining how you praise or revere God from what you learned today.

1. God, I .... you because ....

....

2. God, I .... you because ....

....

3. God, I .... you because ....

....

FOLLOW: Every day gives you the opportunity to follow God more closely and deepen your relationship with him by actively and intentionally experiencing his creation.

In the space below, write down and describe in detail (or draw, color, paint or scrapbook) one or more of the following: something you can see, something you can hear, something you can touch, something you can smell, or something you can taste that you are thankful to God for creating.

CONTINUE THIS PRAYER WITH YOUR OWN CONVERSATION WITH GOD:

Dear God, you are my heavenly Father. Today I come before you to kneel and bow down at your throne. Lord, you are the great God, the great King and Creator of the world, the One who takes care of me. For that Lord, my heart sings for you! I am full of thanksgiving for ....

....

....

....

....

....

.... *Amen.*

NATURE DISCOVERY: Today I added ....
to my nature pocket to remind me of God. I chose it because

....

....

....

....

....

....

....

Day Three

 READ: Begin today by reading Psalm 103 in your Bible.

WRITE: Write Psalm 103:1-5 here:

....

....

....

....

....

....

....

....

....

....

....

....

....

....

LEARN: What do you learn simply and specifically about God and creation's praise of him just from these verses? Write your observations here:

....

....

....

....

....

....

REVERE: Fill in the blanks using a synonym of the word "revere" (admire, adore, appreciate, cherish, exalt, honor, respect, praise, worship) and complete the following sentences explaining how you praise or revere God from what you learned today.

1. God, I .... you because ....

....

2. God, I .... you because ....

....

3. God, I .... you because ....

....

FOLLOW: Every day gives you the opportunity to follow God more closely and deepen your relationship with him by actively and intentionally experiencing his creation.

In the space below, write down and describe in detail (or draw, color, paint or scrapbook) one or more of the following: something you can see, something you can hear, something you can touch, something you can smell, or something you can taste that you are thankful to God for creating.

CONTINUE THIS PRAYER WITH YOUR OWN CONVERSATION WITH GOD:

Dear God, you are my heavenly Father. I was reminded today of all the blessings and benefits that you cover me with. You forgive my sins, you heal my sickness, you redeem my life when I mess up, you crown me with love and compassion, you satisfy me with good things and renew my strength! For all these and

....

....

....

....

....

....*Lord, I praise your holy name! Amen.*

NATURE DISCOVERY: Today I added ....
to my nature pocket to remind me of God. I chose it because

....

....

....

....

....

....

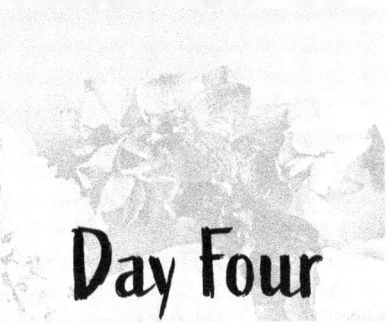

Day Four

 READ: Begin today by reading Psalm 63 in your Bible.

WRITE: Write Psalm 63:1-8 here:

....

....

....

....

....

....

....

....

....

....

....

....

....

....

LEARN: What do you learn simply and specifically about God and creation's praise of him just from these verses? Write your observations here:

....

....

....

....

....

....

REVERE: Fill in the blanks using a synonym of the word "revere" (admire, adore, appreciate, cherish, exalt, honor, respect, praise, worship) and complete the following sentences explaining how you praise or revere God from what you learned today.

1. God, I .... you because ....

....

2. God, I .... you because ....

....

3. God, I .... you because ....

....

FOLLOW: Every day gives you the opportunity to follow God more closely and deepen your relationship with him by actively and intentionally experiencing his creation.

In the space below, write down and describe in detail (or draw, color, paint or scrapbook) one or more of the following: something you can see, something you can hear, something you can touch, something you can smell, or something you can taste that you are thankful to God for creating.

CONTINUE THIS PRAYER WITH YOUR OWN CONVERSATION WITH GOD:

Dear God, you are my heavenly Father. I sing this Psalm to you today because you are my help! I know that only you can satisfy my thirst and fill up my life as no other can. I want to seek you every day; please take my hand and guide me so that ....

....

....

....

....

....

.... *Amen.*

NATURE DISCOVERY: Today I added ....
to my nature pocket to remind me of God. I chose it because

....

....

....

....

....

....

Day Five

 READ: Begin today by reading Psalm 104 and Psalm 105 in your Bible.

WRITE: Write Psalm 104:33-34 and Psalm 105:1-4 here:

....

....

....

....

....

....

....

....

....

....

....

....

....

....

LEARN: What do you learn simply and specifically about God and creation's praise of him just from these verses? Write your observations here:

....

....

....

....

....

....

REVERE: Fill in the blanks using a synonym of the word "revere" (admire, adore, appreciate, cherish, exalt, honor, respect, praise, worship) and complete the following sentences explaining how you praise or revere God from what you learned today.

1. God, I .... you because ....

....

2. God, I .... you because ....

....

3. God, I .... you because ....

....

FOLLOW: Every day gives you the opportunity to follow God more closely and deepen your relationship with him by actively and intentionally experiencing his creation.

In the space below, write down and describe in detail (or draw, color, paint or scrapbook) one or more of the following: something you can see, something you can hear, something you can touch, something you can smell, or something you can taste that you are thankful to God for creating.

CONTINUE THIS PRAYER WITH YOUR OWN CONVERSATION WITH GOD:

Dear God, you are my heavenly Father. My soul becomes so happy when I seek you, when I look to you for strength! Lord, give me courage to tell my little corner of the world all about you; all that you have made and all that you have done in my life. I want to sing to you and praise you for as long as I live. I pray my meditation and songs will be pleasing to you ....

....

....

....

....

....

.... *Amen.*

NATURE DISCOVERY: Today I added ....
to my nature pocket to remind me of God. I chose it because

....

....

....

....

....

....

*I will sing of your love
and justice; to you, Lord,
I will sing praise.*

Psalm 101:1

WEEK FIVE

Heaven's Response:
All of Heaven
Praises God

"The twenty-four elders and the four living creatures fell down and worshiped God, who was seated on the throne. And they cried:

"Amen, Hallelujah!"

Then a voice came from the throne, saying:

"Praise our God, all you his servants, you who fear him, both great and small!" Then I heard what sounded like a great multitude, like the roar of rushing waters and like loud peals of thunder, shouting:

"Hallelujah! For our Lord God Almighty reigns. Let us rejoice and be glad and give him glory! For the wedding of the Lamb has come, and his bride has made herself ready."

Revelation 19:4-7

Day One

READ: Begin today by once again reading Psalm 103 in your Bible.

WRITE: Write Psalm 103:19-22 here:

....

....

....

....

....

....

....

....

....

....

....

....

....

....

LEARN: What do you learn simply and specifically about God and creation's praise of him just from these verses? Write your observations here:

....

....

....

....

....

....

REVERE: Fill in the blanks using a synonym of the word "revere" (admire, adore, appreciate, cherish, exalt, honor, respect, praise, worship) and complete the following sentences explaining how you praise or revere God from what you learned today.

1. God, I .... you because ....

....

2. God, I .... you because ....

....

3. God, I .... you because ....

....

FOLLOW: Every day gives you the opportunity to follow God more closely and deepen your relationship with him by actively and intentionally experiencing his creation.

In the space below, write down and describe in detail (or draw, color, paint or scrapbook) one or more of the following: something you can see, something you can hear, something you can touch, something you can smell, or something you can taste that you are thankful to God for creating.

CONTINUE THIS PRAYER WITH YOUR OWN CONVERSATION WITH GOD:

Dear God, as Mary praised you as recorded in Luke 1:46-48, I praise you! "My soul glorifies the Lord and my spirit rejoices in God my Savior, for he has been mindful of the humble state of his servant." Lord, I am so grateful to be your servant along with all the hosts of heaven! Please open my eyes to see where you need me to serve

....

....

....

....

....

....

.... *Amen.*

NATURE DISCOVERY: Today I added .... to my nature pocket to remind me of God. I chose it because

....

....

....

....

....

....

Day Two

 READ: Begin today by reading Luke 2:1-21 in your Bible.

WRITE: Write Luke 2:8-14 here:

....

....

....

....

....

....

....

....

....

....

....

....

....

....

LEARN: What do you learn simply and specifically about God and creation's praise of him just from these verses? Write your observations here:

....

....

....

....

....

....

REVERE: Fill in the blanks using a synonym of the word "revere" (admire, adore, appreciate, cherish, exalt, honor, respect, praise, worship) and complete the following sentences explaining how you praise or revere God from what you learned today.

1. God, I .... you because ....

....

2. God, I .... you because ....

....

3. God, I .... you because ....

....

FOLLOW: Every day gives you the opportunity to follow God more closely and deepen your relationship with him by actively and intentionally experiencing his creation.

In the space below, write down and describe in detail (or draw, color, paint or scrapbook) one or more of the following: something you can see, something you can hear, something you can touch, something you can smell, or something you can taste that you are thankful to God for creating.

CONTINUE THIS PRAYER WITH YOUR OWN CONVERSATION WITH GOD:

Dear God, thank you for the good news that was first proclaimed by the angels to the shepherds! Thank you for sending your Son to be my Savior. I praise you with all the heavenly host...Glory to God in the highest! May all glory and praise go to you for loving me so much. ....

....

....

....

....

....

....

.... *Amen.*

NATURE DISCOVERY: Today I added ....
to my nature pocket to remind me of God. I chose it because

....

....

....

....

....

....

Day Three

 READ: Begin today by reading Revelation 4 in your Bible.

WRITE: Write Revelation 4:8-11 here:

....

....

....

....

....

....

....

....

....

....

....

....

....

....

LEARN: What do you learn simply and specifically about God and creation's praise of him just from these verses? Write your observations here:

....

....

....

....

....

....

REVERE: Fill in the blanks using a synonym of the word "revere" (admire, adore, appreciate, cherish, exalt, honor, respect, praise, worship) and complete the following sentences explaining how you praise or revere God from what you learned today.

1. God, I .... you because ....

....

2. God, I .... you because ....

....

3. God, I .... you because ....

....

FOLLOW: Every day gives you the opportunity to follow God more closely and deepen your relationship with him by actively and intentionally experiencing his creation.

In the space below, write down and describe in detail (or draw, color, paint or scrapbook) one or more of the following: something you can see, something you can hear, something you can touch, something you can smell, or something you can taste that you are thankful to God for creating.

CONTINUE THIS PRAYER WITH YOUR OWN CONVERSATION WITH GOD:

Dear God, today my prayer comes from Revelation 4:8 and 11, "Holy, holy, holy is the Lord God Almighty, who was, and is, and is to come... You are worthy, our Lord and God, to receive glory and honor and power, for you created all things, and by your will they were created and have their being." I worship you; I bow before you ....

....

....

....

....

....

.... *Amen.*

NATURE DISCOVERY: Today I added ....
to my nature pocket to remind me of God. I chose it because

....

....

....

....

....

....

Day Four

READ: Begin today by reading Revelation 5 in your Bible.

WRITE: Write Revelation 5:11-14 here:

....

....

....

....

....

....

....

....

....

....

....

....

....

....

LEARN: What do you learn simply and specifically about God and creation's praise of him just from these verses? Write your observations here:

....

....

....

....

....

....

REVERE: Fill in the blanks using a synonym of the word "revere" (admire, adore, appreciate, cherish, exalt, honor, respect, praise, worship) and complete the following sentences explaining how you praise or revere God from what you learned today.

1. God, I .... you because ....

....

2. God, I .... you because ....

....

3. God, I .... you because ....

....

FOLLOW: Every day gives you the opportunity to follow God more closely and deepen your relationship with him by actively and intentionally experiencing his creation.

In the space below, write down and describe in detail (or draw, color, paint or scrapbook) one or more of the following: something you can see, something you can hear, something you can touch, something you can smell, or something you can taste that you are thankful to God for creating.

CONTINUE THIS PRAYER WITH YOUR OWN CONVERSATION WITH GOD:

Dear God, today I begin my prayer with these words from Revelation 5:12-13, "Worthy is the Lamb, who was slain, to receive power and wealth and wisdom and strength and honor and glory and praise... To him who sits on the throne and to the Lamb be praise and honor and glory and power, for ever and ever!"

....

....

....

....

....

....

.... *Amen.*

NATURE DISCOVERY: Today I added ....
to my nature pocket to remind me of God. I chose it because

....

....

....

....

....

....

Day Five

 READ: Begin today by reading Revelation 7:9-17 in your Bible.

WRITE: Write Revelation 7:11-12 here:

....

....

....

....

....

....

....

....

....

....

....

....

....

LEARN: What do you learn simply and specifically about God and creation's praise of him just from these verses? Write your observations here:

....

....

....

....

....

....

REVERE: Fill in the blanks using a synonym of the word "revere" (admire, adore, appreciate, cherish, exalt, honor, respect, praise, worship) and complete the following sentences explaining how you praise or revere God from what you learned today.

1. God, I .... you because ....

....

2. God, I .... you because ....

....

3. God, I .... you because ....

....

FOLLOW: Every day gives you the opportunity to follow God more closely and deepen your relationship with him by actively and intentionally experiencing his creation.

In the space below, write down and describe in detail (or draw, color, paint or scrapbook) one or more of the following: something you can see, something you can hear, something you can touch, something you can smell, or something you can taste that you are thankful to God for creating.

CONTINUE THIS PRAYER WITH YOUR OWN CONVERSATION WITH GOD:

Dear God, this week I have read and seen how all of heaven worships and praises you because of who you are. It is incredible for me to read about your throne in Revelation and all those that surround you. I wonder, who am I to be worthy to join them? Then I remember I am your child; you are my Father and you love me. Therefore, with all the heavenly hosts in Revelation 7:12, I also say, "Amen! Praise and glory and wisdom and thanks and honor and power and strength be to our God for ever and ever ....

....

....

....

....

....

.... *Amen.*

NATURE DISCOVERY: Today I added .... to my nature pocket to remind me of God. I chose it because

....

....

....

....

....

....

Sing joyfully to the Lord, you righteous; it is fitting for the upright to praise him.

Psalm 33:1

WEEK SIX

God Takes Delight in His Creation

"God saw all that he had made, and it was very good. And there was evening, and there was morning - the sixth day. Thus the heavens and the earth were completed in all their vast array. By the seventh day God had finished the work he had been doing; so on the seventh day he rested from all his work. Then God blessed the seventh day and made it holy, because on it he rested from all the work of creating that he had done."

Genesis 1:31-2:3

Day One

 **READ:** Begin today by reading Psalm 37 in your Bible.

WRITE: Write Psalm 37:23-24 here:

....

....

....

....

....

....

....

....

....

....

....

....

....

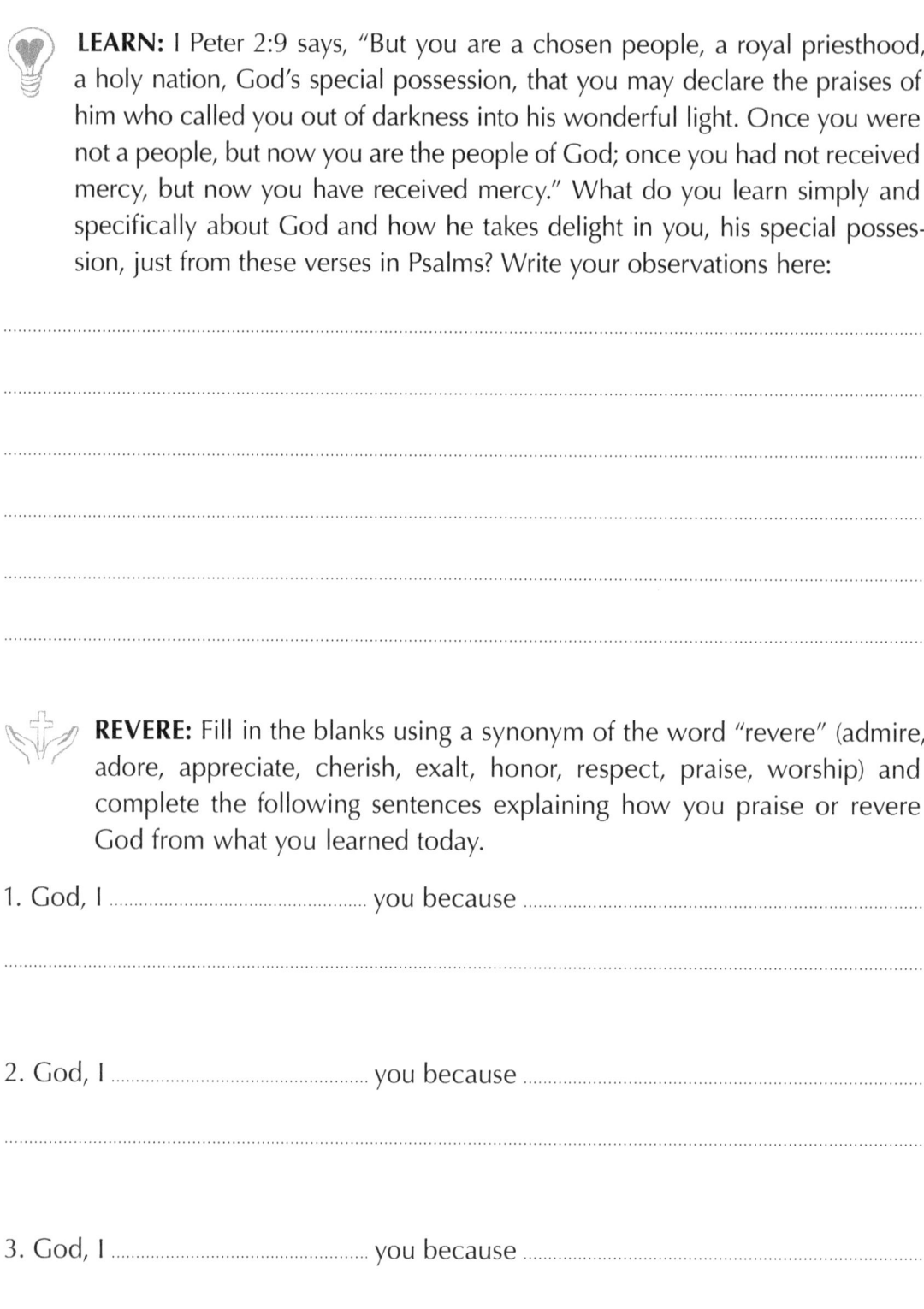

LEARN: I Peter 2:9 says, "But you are a chosen people, a royal priesthood, a holy nation, God's special possession, that you may declare the praises of him who called you out of darkness into his wonderful light. Once you were not a people, but now you are the people of God; once you had not received mercy, but now you have received mercy." What do you learn simply and specifically about God and how he takes delight in you, his special possession, just from these verses in Psalms? Write your observations here:

....

....

....

....

....

....

REVERE: Fill in the blanks using a synonym of the word "revere" (admire, adore, appreciate, cherish, exalt, honor, respect, praise, worship) and complete the following sentences explaining how you praise or revere God from what you learned today.

1. God, I .... you because ....

....

2. God, I .... you because ....

....

3. God, I .... you because ....

....

FOLLOW: Every day gives you the opportunity to follow God more closely and deepen your relationship with him by actively and intentionally experiencing his creation.

In the space below, write down and describe in detail (or draw, color, paint or scrapbook) one or more of the following: something you can see, something you can hear, something you can touch, something you can smell, or something you can taste that you are thankful to God for creating.

CONTINUE THIS PRAYER WITH YOUR OWN CONVERSATION WITH GOD:

Dear God, thank you for holding me up and not letting me stumble and fall as long as I hold onto you! This passage today reminds me of a similar one from your prophet Isaiah in Isaiah 40:28-31 "Do you not know? Have you not heard? The Lord is the everlasting God, the Creator of the ends of the earth. He will not grow tired or weary, and his understanding no one can fathom. He gives strength to the weary and increases the power of the weak. Even youths grow tired and weary, and young men stumble and fall; but those who hope in the Lord will renew their strength. They will soar on wings like eagles; they will run and not grow weary, they will walk and not be faint." I pray, Lord, that you do find delight in me as you walk by my side day after day. I pray that you will make my steps firm

....

....

....

....

.... *Amen.*

NATURE DISCOVERY: Today I added .... to my nature pocket to remind me of God. I chose it because

....

....

....

....

....

Day Two

 READ: Begin today by reading Psalm 147 and Psalm 149 in your Bible.

WRITE: Write Psalm 147:11 and 149:4 here:

....

....

....

....

....

....

....

....

....

....

....

....

....

....

LEARN: I Peter 2:9 says, "But you are a chosen people, a royal priesthood, a holy nation, God's special possession, that you may declare the praises of him who called you out of darkness into his wonderful light. Once you were not a people, but now you are the people of God; once you had not received mercy, but now you have received mercy." What do you learn simply and specifically about God and how he takes delight in you, his special possession, just from these verses in Psalms? Write your observations here:

....

....

....

....

....

....

REVERE: Fill in the blanks using a synonym of the word "revere" (admire, adore, appreciate, cherish, exalt, honor, respect, praise, worship) and complete the following sentences explaining how you praise or revere God from what you learned today.

1. God, I .... you because ....

....

2. God, I .... you because ....

....

3. God, I .... you because ....

....

FOLLOW: Every day gives you the opportunity to follow God more closely and deepen your relationship with him by actively and intentionally experiencing his creation.

In the space below, write down and describe in detail (or draw, color, paint or scrapbook) one or more of the following: something you can see, something you can hear, something you can touch, something you can smell, or something you can taste that you are thankful to God for creating.

CONTINUE THIS PRAYER WITH YOUR OWN CONVERSATION WITH GOD:

Dear God, as the psalmist says on many occasions, how good and pleasant and fitting it is to sing praises to you! I put my hope and trust in you, my Savior and my God. Thank you for protecting me, for strengthening me and providing me with

....

....

....

....

....

....

....*Amen.*

NATURE DISCOVERY: Today I added .... to my nature pocket to remind me of God. I chose it because

....

....

....

....

....

....

Day Three

 READ: Begin today by reading Jeremiah 9:23-24 in your Bible.

WRITE: Write Jeremiah 9:23-24 here:

....

....

....

....

....

....

....

....

....

....

....

....

....

....

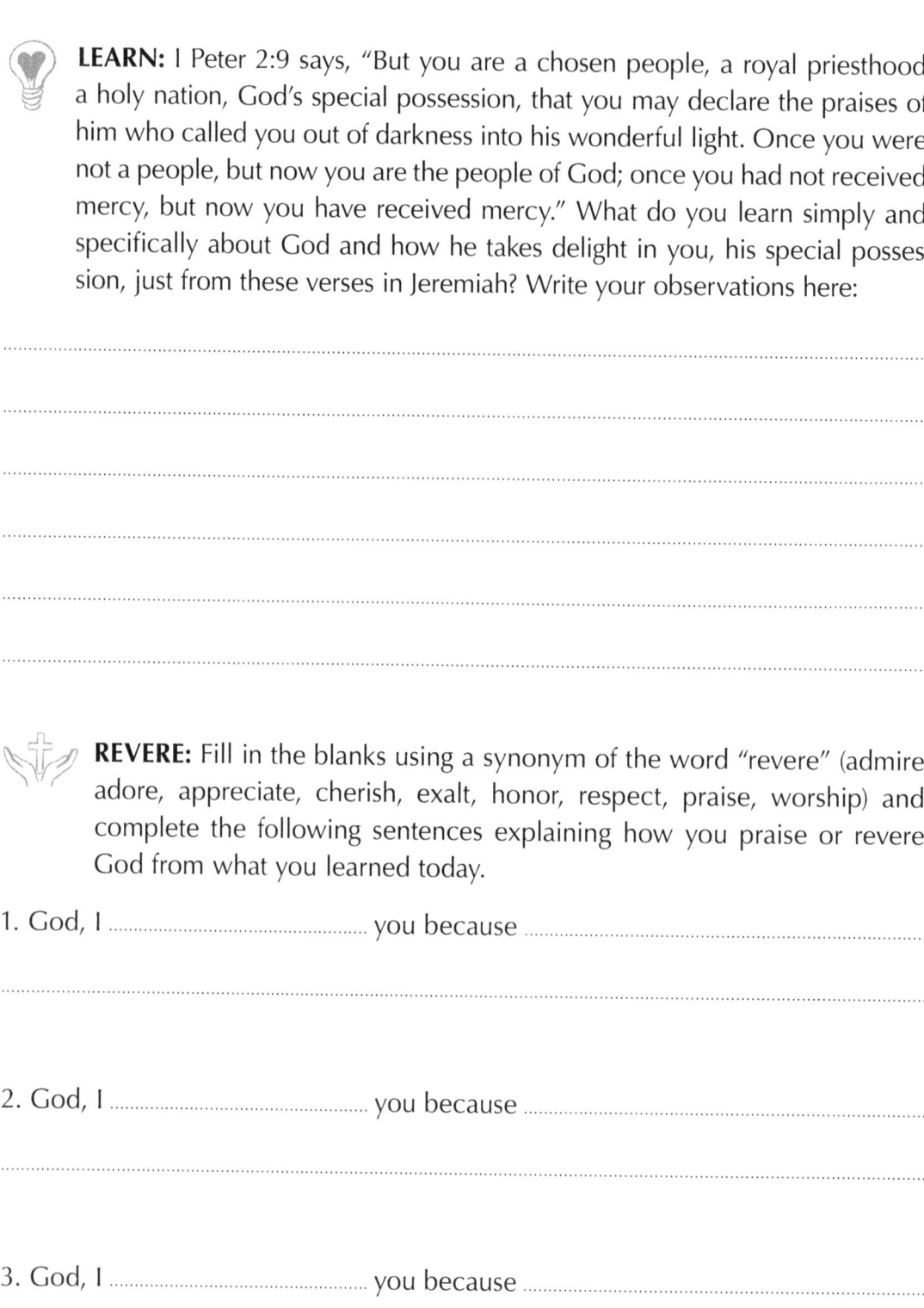

LEARN: I Peter 2:9 says, "But you are a chosen people, a royal priesthood, a holy nation, God's special possession, that you may declare the praises of him who called you out of darkness into his wonderful light. Once you were not a people, but now you are the people of God; once you had not received mercy, but now you have received mercy." What do you learn simply and specifically about God and how he takes delight in you, his special possession, just from these verses in Jeremiah? Write your observations here:

....

....

....

....

....

....

REVERE: Fill in the blanks using a synonym of the word "revere" (admire, adore, appreciate, cherish, exalt, honor, respect, praise, worship) and complete the following sentences explaining how you praise or revere God from what you learned today.

1. God, I .... you because ....

....

2. God, I .... you because ....

....

3. God, I .... you because ....

....

FOLLOW: Every day gives you the opportunity to follow God more closely and deepen your relationship with him by actively and intentionally experiencing his creation.

In the space below, write down and describe in detail (or draw, color, paint or scrapbook) one or more of the following: something you can see, something you can hear, something you can touch, something you can smell, or something you can taste that you are thankful to God for creating.

CONTINUE THIS PRAYER WITH YOUR OWN CONVERSATION WITH GOD:

Dear God, thank you for giving me your word so that I may come to know you. Thank you for the wonders of creation that point to you every day. Please help me to be like you, to exercise kindness, justice, and righteousness to those around me

....

....

....

....

....

....

....*Amen.*

NATURE DISCOVERY: Today I added ....
to my nature pocket to remind me of God. I chose it because

....

....

....

....

....

....

Day Four

 READ: Begin today by reading John 3:1-21 in your Bible.

WRITE: Write John 3:16-17 here:

....

....

....

....

....

....

....

....

....

....

....

....

....

....

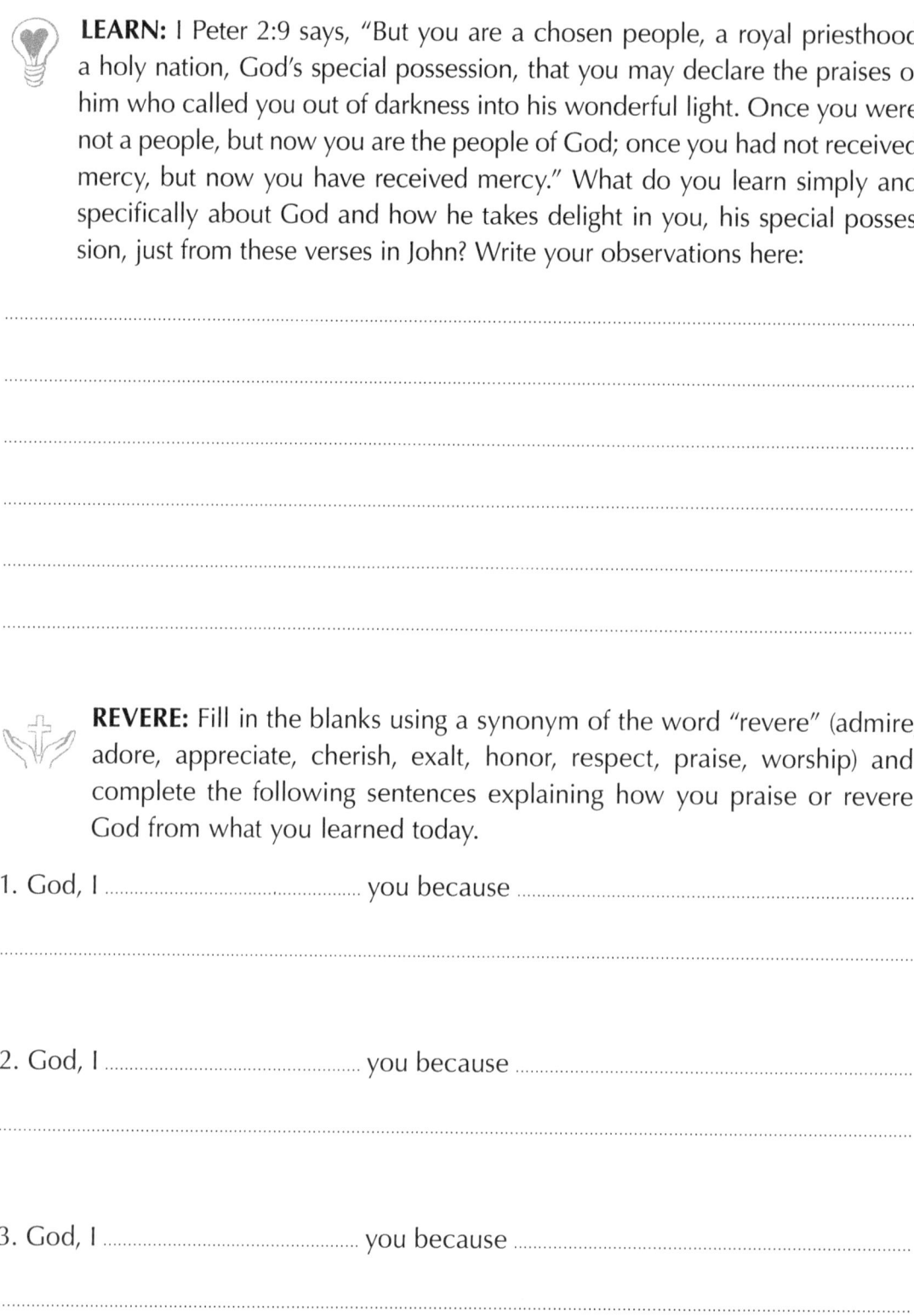

LEARN: I Peter 2:9 says, "But you are a chosen people, a royal priesthood, a holy nation, God's special possession, that you may declare the praises of him who called you out of darkness into his wonderful light. Once you were not a people, but now you are the people of God; once you had not received mercy, but now you have received mercy." What do you learn simply and specifically about God and how he takes delight in you, his special possession, just from these verses in John? Write your observations here:

....

....

....

....

....

....

REVERE: Fill in the blanks using a synonym of the word "revere" (admire, adore, appreciate, cherish, exalt, honor, respect, praise, worship) and complete the following sentences explaining how you praise or revere God from what you learned today.

1. God, I .... you because ....

....

2. God, I .... you because ....

....

3. God, I .... you because ....

....

FOLLOW: Every day gives you the opportunity to follow God more closely and deepen your relationship with him by actively and intentionally experiencing his creation.

In the space below, write down and describe in detail (or draw, color, paint or scrapbook) one or more of the following: something you can see, something you can hear, something you can touch, something you can smell, or something you can taste that you are thankful to God for creating.

CONTINUE THIS PRAYER WITH YOUR OWN CONVERSATION WITH GOD:

Dear God, thank you for sending your Son into the world so that someone like me could have the opportunity to spend eternity with you ....

....

....

....

....

....

....

.... *Amen.*

NATURE DISCOVERY: Today I added ....
to my nature pocket to remind me of God. I chose it because

....

....

....

....

....

....

Day Five

 READ: Begin today by reading Zephaniah 3:14-17 in your Bible.

WRITE: Write Zephaniah 3:14-17 here:

....

....

....

....

....

....

....

....

....

....

....

....

....

....

LEARN: I Peter 2:9 says, "But you are a chosen people, a royal priesthood, a holy nation, God's special possession, that you may declare the praises of him who called you out of darkness into his wonderful light. Once you were not a people, but now you are the people of God; once you had not received mercy, but now you have received mercy." What do you learn simply and specifically about God and how he takes delight in you, his special possession, just from these verses in Zephaniah? Write your observations here:

....

....

....

....

....

....

REVERE: Fill in the blanks using a synonym of the word "revere" (admire, adore, appreciate, cherish, exalt, honor, respect, praise, worship) and complete the following sentences explaining how you praise or revere God from what you learned today.

1. God, I .... you because ....

....

2. God, I .... you because ....

....

3. God, I .... you because ....

....

FOLLOW: Every day gives you the opportunity to follow God more closely and deepen your relationship with him by actively and intentionally experiencing his creation.

In the space below, write down and describe in detail (or draw, color, paint or scrapbook) one or more of the following: something you can see, something you can hear, something you can touch, something you can smell, or something you can taste that you are thankful to God for creating.

CONTINUE THIS PRAYER WITH YOUR OWN CONVERSATION WITH GOD:

Dear God, it gives me such comfort and peace to know that you rejoice over me with singing! As I come to the end of these thirty days spent journaling through creation with you, I praise you for all of creation. I thank you for accepting my worship. Please help me to keep my eyes open to what you have made, my ears ready to hear both your song and creation's song, and my spirit more in tune with you

....

....

....

....

....

....

.... *Amen.*

NATURE DISCOVERY: Today I added .... to my nature pocket to remind me of God. I chose it because

....

....

....

....

....

....

Conclusion

Dear Reader,

Thank you so much for joining me on this journey of exploring creation and discovering creation's response to God. It's my prayer that these last 30 days have uplifted your spirit and drawn your soul closer to the One who made you. Whether you have filled this journal with your descriptive words or colorful artwork, or filled your nature pocket with pressed flowers, shells, or pinecones, may they be an encouragement and reminder to you in the future of just how much your Creator loves you and longs to have a holy relationship with you!

Blessings in Christ,

Robin

SPECIAL THANKS TO

My family – your encouragement always fills my heart with joy!

Flourish Writers – Mindy and Jenny, you helped me transform my dream into reality.

Allen Arnold – your daily inspirations in my inbox kept my focus on creating with my Creator.

My heavenly Father – I love creating with you.

About the Author

Robin Simpson loves living her dream of serving in ministry alongside her husband and best friend, Gary. They have three wonderful children who are just beginning their adult life adventures with God. Besides being a preacher's wife, mom, and school teacher, she enjoys teaching Bible classes, journaling Scripture, and exploring the great outdoors. Her favorite experiences in nature include the sound of water gurgling over rocks in the river, the smell of fresh rain, and the taste of a plump apricot picked fresh from the tree.

If you have enjoyed this Bible study adventure and would like to discover more ways to journal through Scripture, visit Robin at www.calledtobehis.com or click on the code below!

Use these pages to try out your markers, pens, paints, etc.

Be

Creative

Be

Creative

Be
Creative

Be

Creative

Be

Creative